FIRST 50 SOLOS

YOU SHOULD PLAY ON THE SNARE DRUM

Compiled by Ben Hans

ISBN 978-1-5400-2762-7

Visit Hal Leonard Online at
www.halleonard.com

Contact us:
Hal Leonard
7777 West Bluemound Road
Milwaukee, WI 53213
Email: info@halleonard.com

In Europe, contact:
Hal Leonard Europe Limited
42 Wigmore Street
Marylebone, London, W1U 2RN
Email: info@halleonardeurope.com

In Australia, contact:
Hal Leonard Australia Pty. Ltd.
4 Lentara Court
Cheltenham, Victoria, 3192 Australia
Email: info@halleonard.com.au

CONTENTS

NOTATION LEGEND

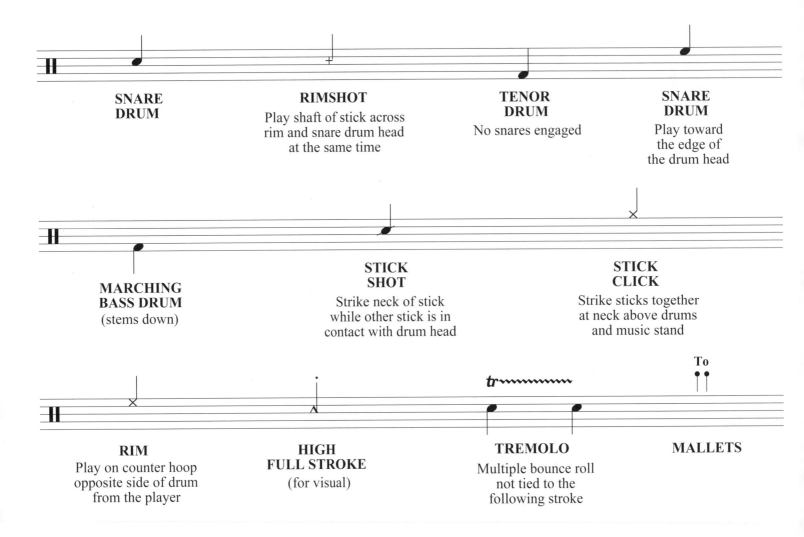

SNARE DRUM

RIMSHOT
Play shaft of stick across rim and snare drum head at the same time

TENOR DRUM
No snares engaged

SNARE DRUM
Play toward the edge of the drum head

MARCHING BASS DRUM
(stems down)

STICK SHOT
Strike neck of stick while other stick is in contact with drum head

STICK CLICK
Strike sticks together at neck above drums and music stand

RIM
Play on counter hoop opposite side of drum from the player

HIGH FULL STROKE
(for visual)

TREMOLO
Multiple bounce roll not tied to the following stroke

MALLETS

NORWEGIAN DANCE
Opus 35, No. 2

EDVARD GRIEG
Arranged by James Curnow

TURKISH MARCH

LUDWIG VAN BEETHOVEN
Arranged by Ann Lindsay

WILLIAM TELL OVERTURE

GIOACCHINO ROSSINI
Arranged by James Curnow

BOLÉRO

MAURICE RAVEL

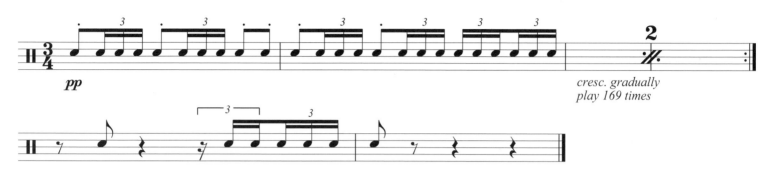

cresc. gradually
play 169 times

UPSTAIRS/DOWNSTAIRS

BEN HANS

MARCH FOR TWO DRUMS

MORRIS GOLDENBERG

11

DANZA DYNAMICO

GERT BOMHOF

SIMPLE MINUET

MORRIS GOLDENBERG

EIGHT-PARADE

GERT BOMHOF

* = *Stick Shot*

STUDY #2

FRANK COLONNATO

This study in 7/8 is based on a 3 + 4 subdivision, or 3 + 2 + 2.

STUDY #6

FRANK COLONNATO

Play this 9/8 piece in a relaxed "three" feel throughout.

MR. ROTHMAN'S MARCH

Dedicated to Joel Rothman of London, England, percussion instructor and author

BEN HANS

FARFEL'S GAVOTTE

MORRIS GOLDENBERG

SOLDIER'S MARCH

MORRIS GOLDENBERG

GRADUATION ETUDE

MORRIS GOLDENBERG

PEARL HARBOR SUITE

Dedicated to the veterans of WWII Pacific Theatre

BEN HANS

Mvt. I Prelude to a Storm

Mvt. II Day of Infamy

Mvt. III From Arizona to Missouri

TIJUANA TAP

BEN HANS

ÉTUDE #2

JACQUES DELÉCLUSE

ÉTUDE #7

JACQUES DELÉCLUSE

ÉTUDE #5

JACQUES DELÉCLUSE

34

ÉTUDE #8

JACQUES DELÉCUSE

RUDIMENTAL RHUMBA

CRAIG ALAN

DOWNFALL OF PARIS

TRADITIONAL
(1790)

* Stylistically, in traditional rudimental drumming, these rolls are "squeezed" into the time space of the next smaller roll
(i.e. the 7-stroke roll in the time space of a 5-stroke roll, and the 15-stroke roll in the time space of a 13-stroke roll).

THREE CAMPS
(in Modern Triplet Notation)

TRADITIONAL

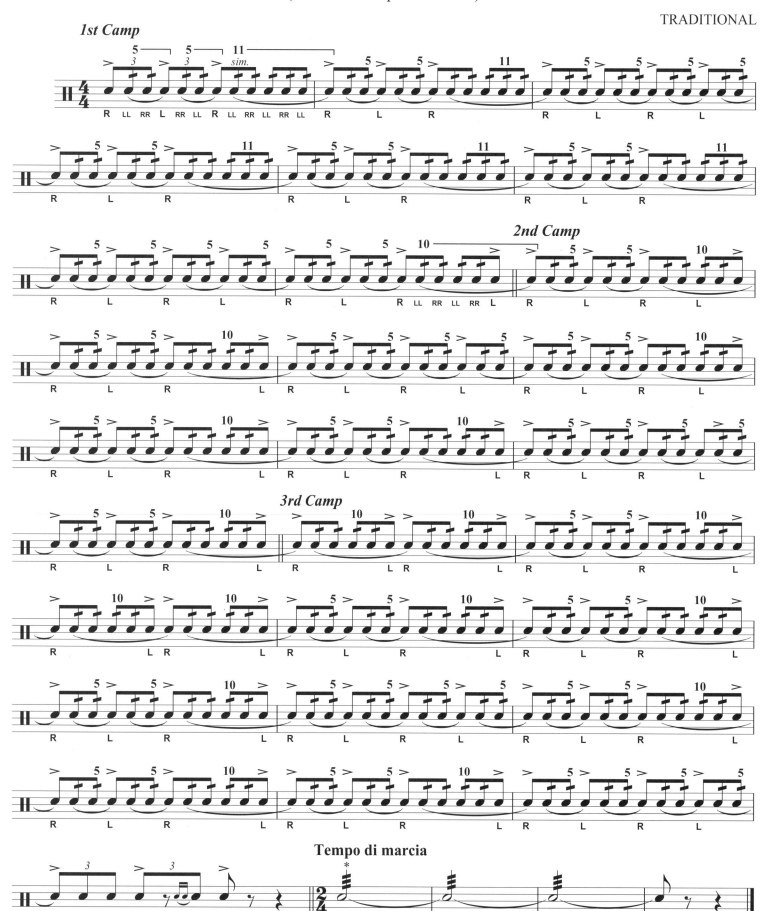

*Traditionally, the roll was used to break up the different pieces in the Reveille.
It should not be subdivided as triplets but rather played as a normal 16th-note based roll.*

THE GENERAL

TRADITIONAL

GRANDFATHER'S CLOCK

HENRY CLAY WORK

CRAZY ARMY

from the Company of Fifers & Drummers Music Books, Vol. 1 & II

ED LEMLEY

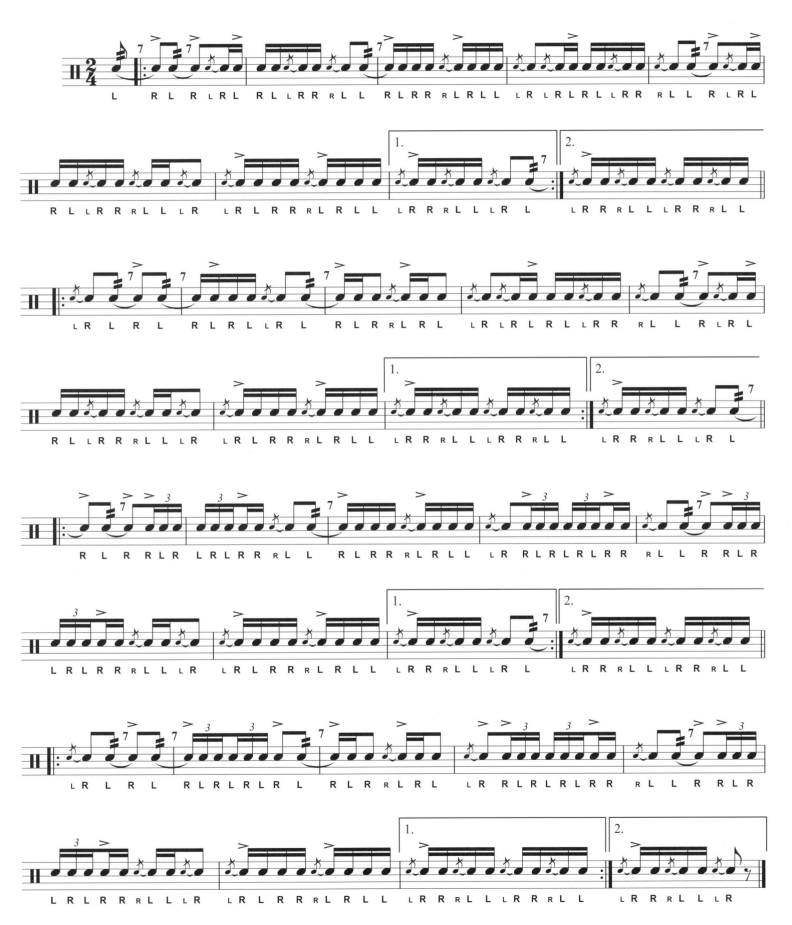

CONNECTICUT HALFTIME

Attributed to
J. BURNS MOORE

1st Filling

2nd Filling

* Dynamics can and should be added at the discretion of the performer.

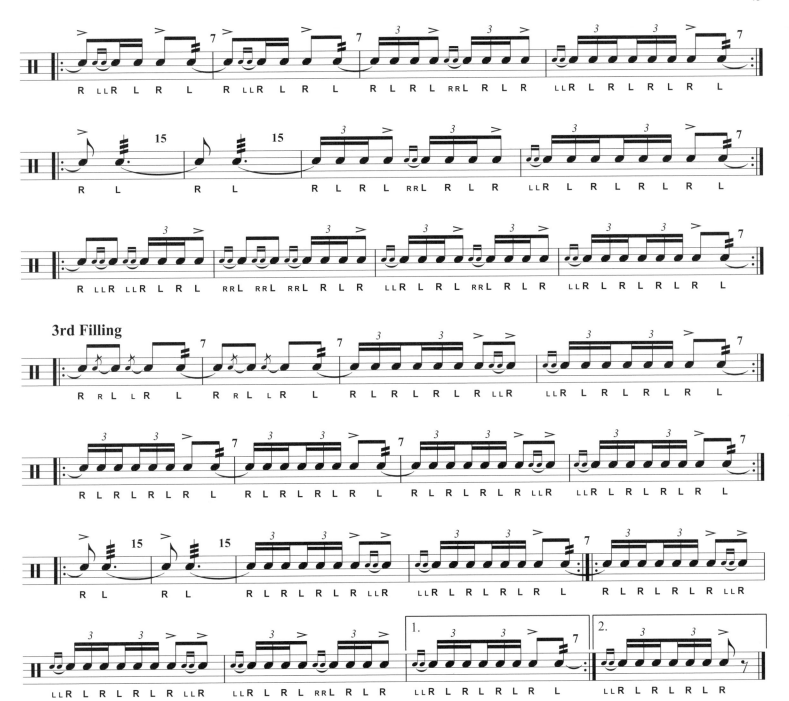

3rd Filling

ECHOING STICKS

R.W. BUGGERT

ROLLING ACCENTS

R.M. BUGGERT

* Continuous roll but make the accents as single stroke.

BOBBIN' BACK

R.W. BUGGERT

NEWGULF DRUMMER

A.H. KELLY

CAPTAIN WHITINGS

HASKELL W. HARR

COL. ANDREWS

HASKELL W. HARR

BUNKER HILL

HASKELL W. HARR

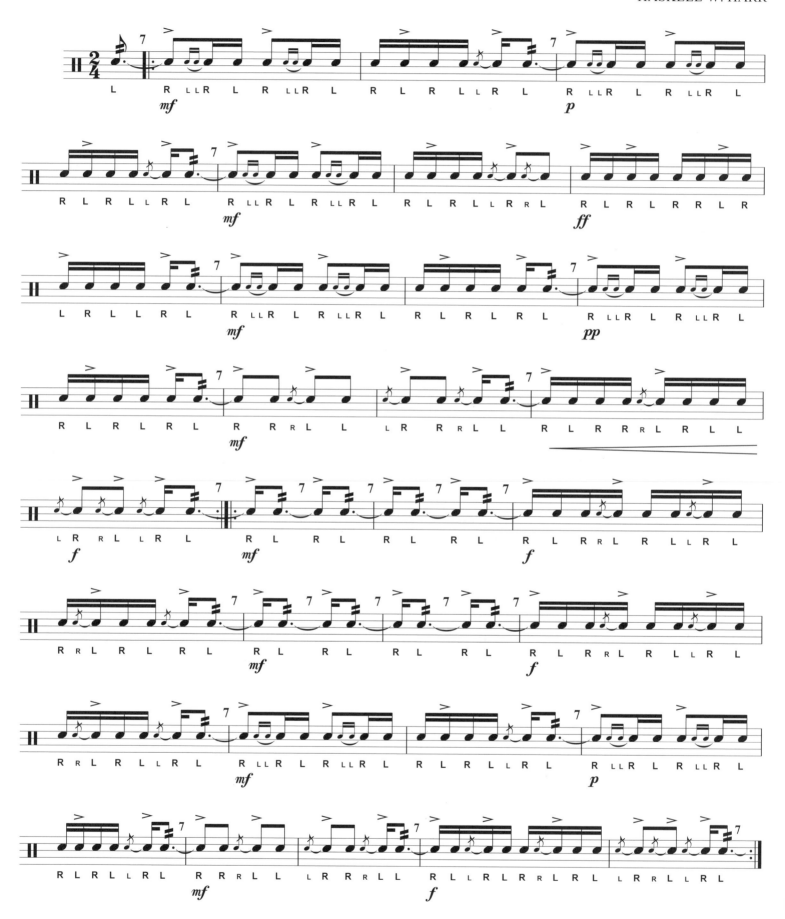

THE GLENWOOD BOY

HASKELL W. HARR

MEMORIAL DAY PARADE

Dedicated to the United States military personnel lost in Foreign Wars

BEN HANS

THE RIGHT TOUCH

SPERIE KARAS

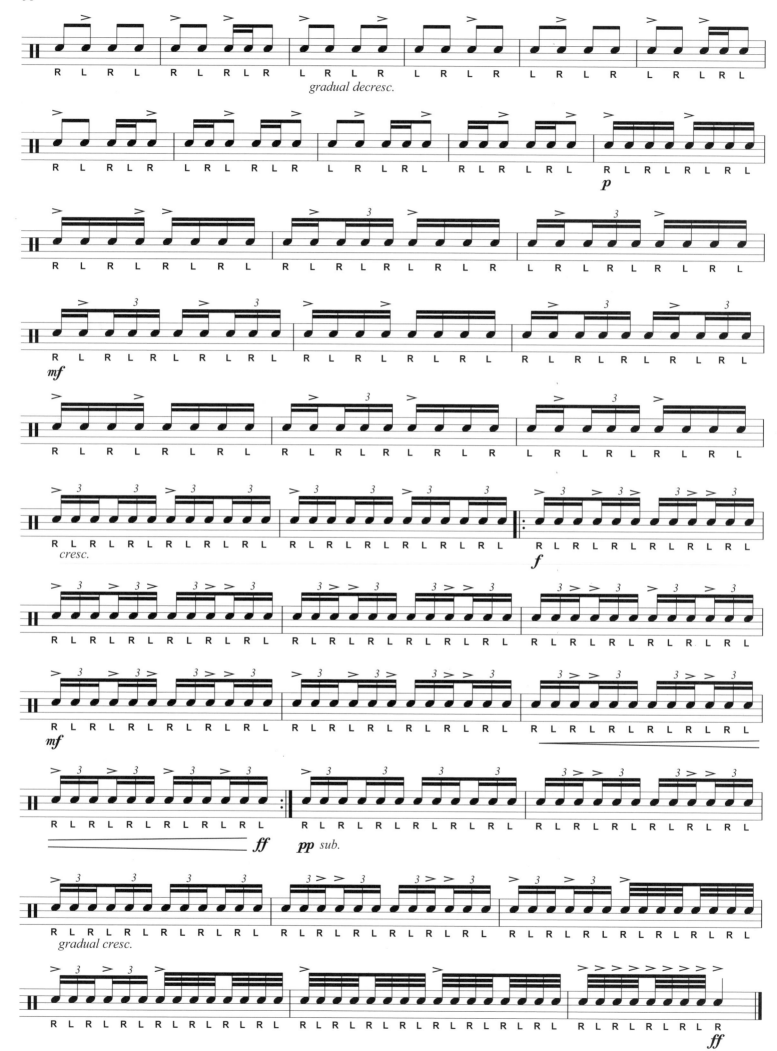

SCOUT'S HONOR

Written for Jeff Reed of the Young Colonials, a longtime Scout and drummer.
His dedication to both activities is an inspiration to everyone who knows him!

GUS CUCCIA JR.

ROLLIN' AND ROCKIN'

SPERIE KARAS

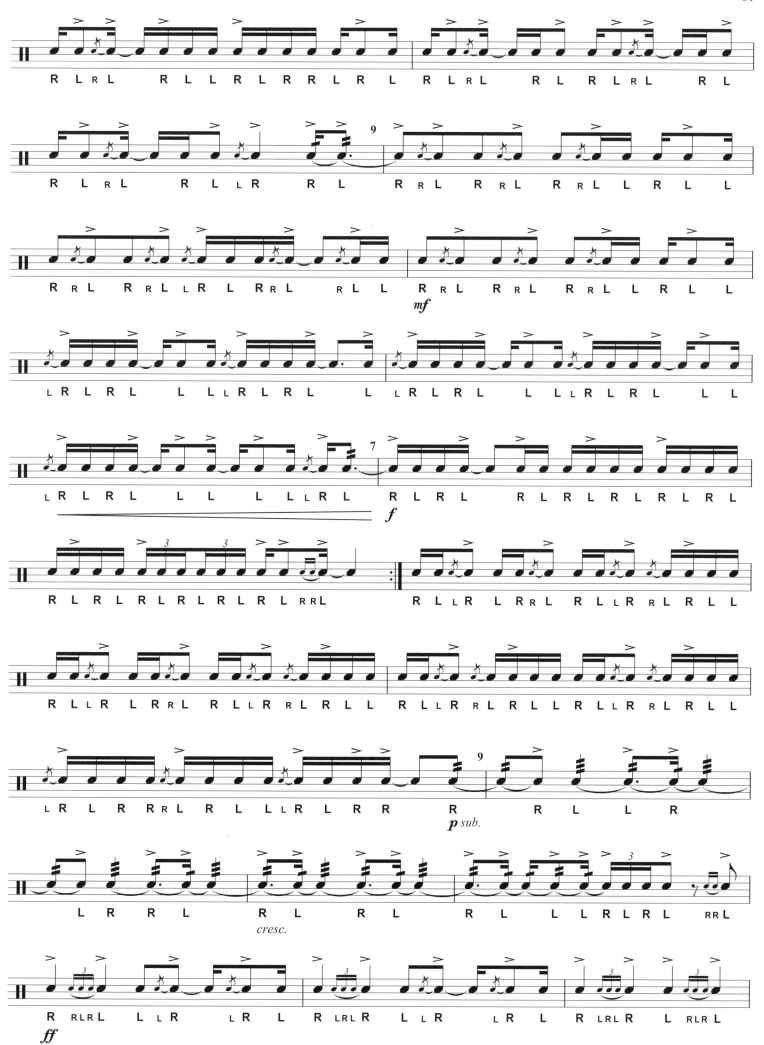

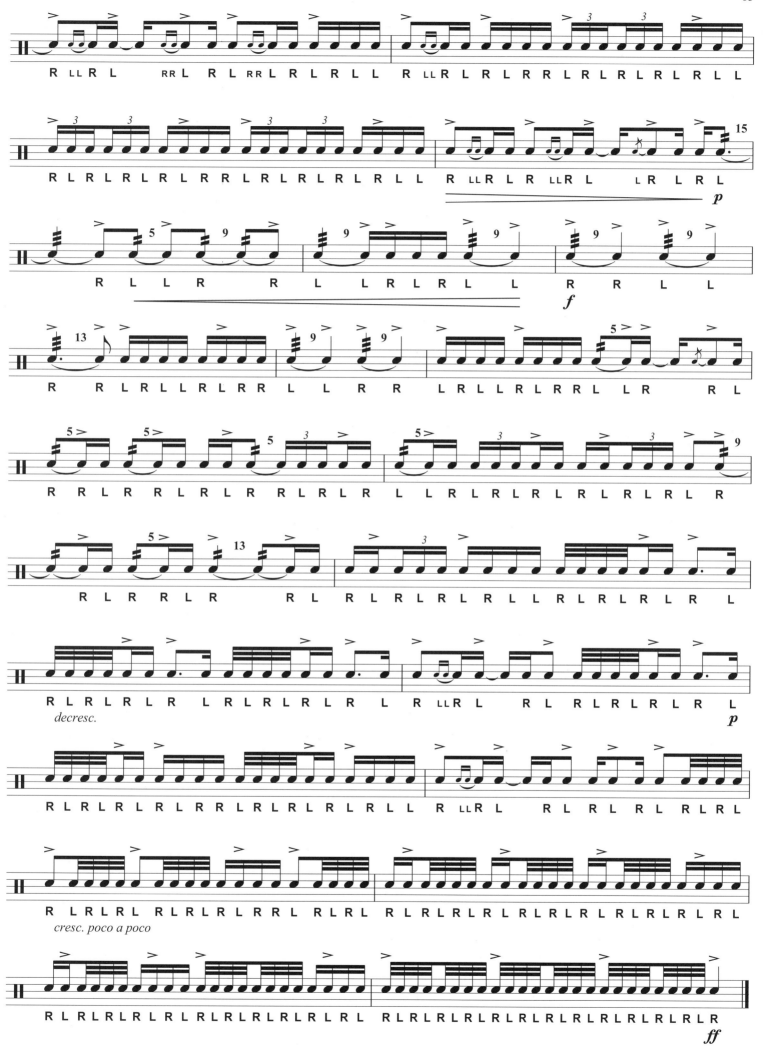

JUST FEELING THE FLAMACUE

Dedicated to Kyle Fitzsimons, grandson of the composer

JOHN S. PRATT

DOUBLE PARADIDDLE THUMPSTER

Dedicated to Jeff Salisbury, percussion instructor, the University of Vermont

JOHN S. PRATT

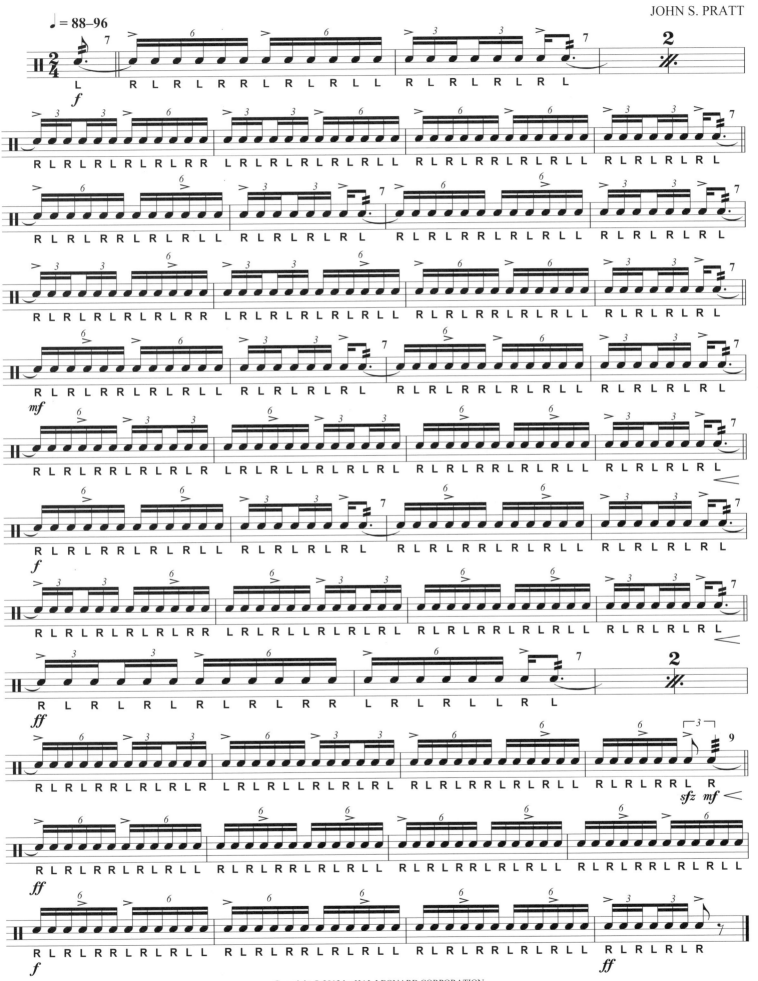

LITTLE TOY DRUM

JOHN S. PRATT

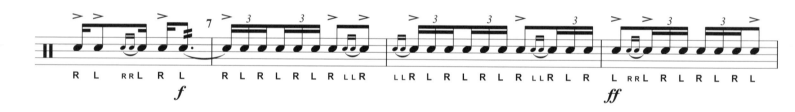

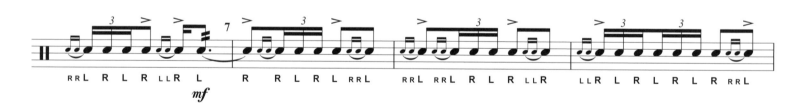

INTERSTATESMAN A.B.C./1962

To C.A.D.R.E. with Best Regards

JOHN S. PRATT

B

STANDING ON THE SHOULDERS OF GIANTS

Dedicated to John S. "Jack" Pratt and the International Association of Traditional Drummers

BEN HANS

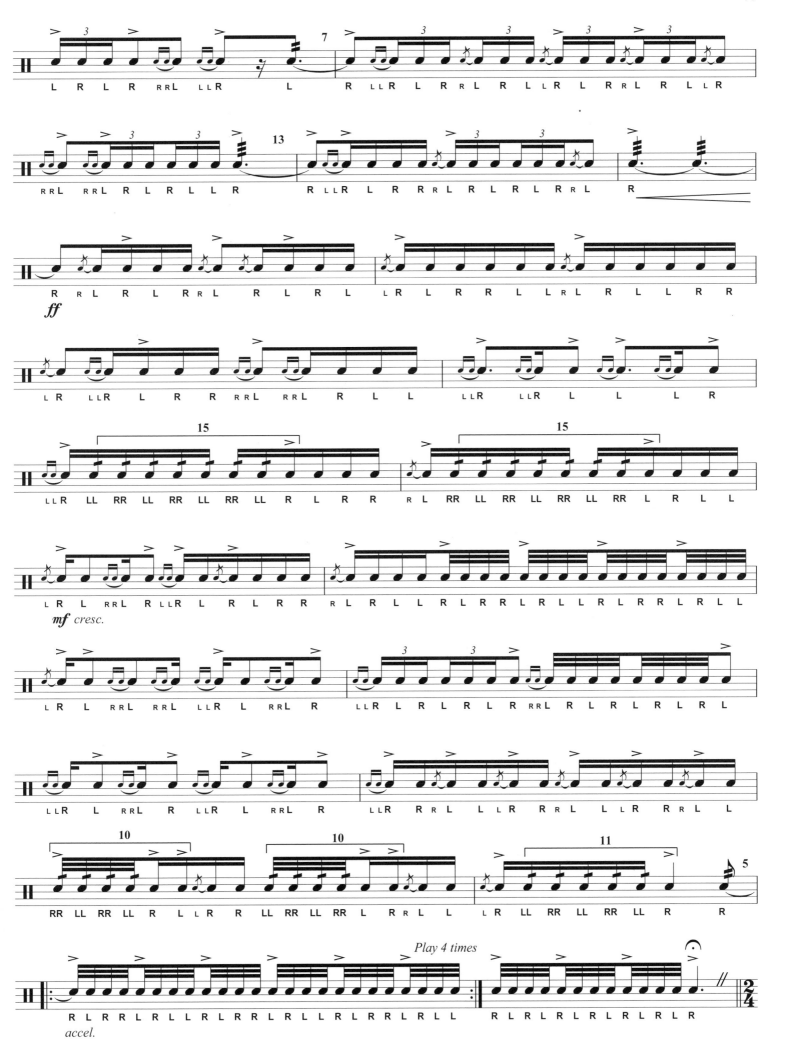

PERFORMANCE TIPS

- Each movement of this solo contains a complete set of the standard 26 (N.A.R.D.) American Drum Rudiments. Can you find them?
- In the measure before D.S., build a single stroke roll to your top speed. When finished, proceed to a double stroke roll, and hold until D.S. (no seven stroke roll pickup).

SWISS CRAZY ARMY
Variant 1
Dedicated to Alex Duthart of Scotland

JOHN S. PRATT

THE BEACH

Dedicated to the brave men who landed on the beaches of Normandy on D-Day, June 6th, 1944

BEN HANS

THE AUSTIN ARMY

For Therese Cuccia, Rick Jones, Brendan Mason and Mark Reilly

DOMINICK CUCCIA

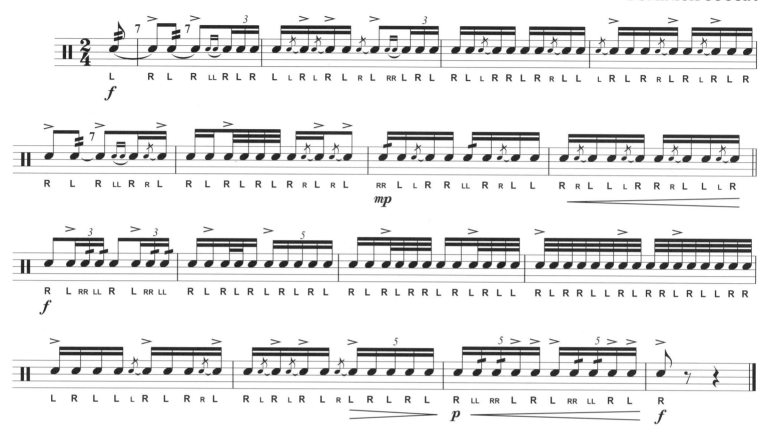

Author's Note

For my clinic at PASIC 2008 in Austin, Texas, I asked Therese, Rick, Brendan and Mark to join me as a group I referred to as "The Not-So-Traditional Players." What an honor it was to make music with the four of them. We had all drummed together in the past, but this was our first opportunity to take the stage for an hour and it was an incredible experience for all of us. **The Austin Army** was written specifically for the show and is a variation of Ed Lemley's classic drum solo, **Crazy Army**.

LOVE THOSE TRIPLETS & FLAS

For Jeff Paradise

DOMINICK CUCCIA

Author's Note

Jeff was a friend with the Young Colonials who showed me a rudiment he referred to as "one-handed flam taps." As it turned out, that rudiment was already known as the "Swiss Army Triplet." In turn, I shared one of my favorites with him, the "Pataflafla." I thought it would be cool to combine the two in a 16-bar solo/exercise. This was written a long time ago, hasn't been seen by many, has been edited a few times and was one of the first things I ever wrote. Jeff & I shared in our discovery of all that drumming has to offer, and this piece is a tribute to the joy that all young drummers experience as they learn this beautiful language of music.

GET "RICH" QUICK

DOMINICK CUCCIA

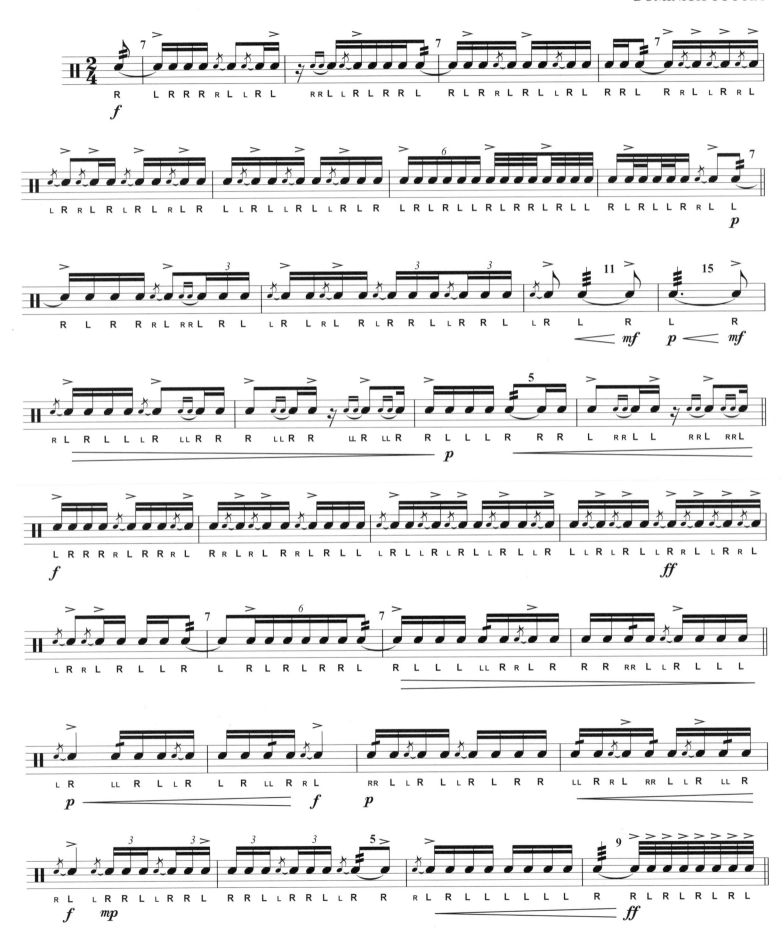

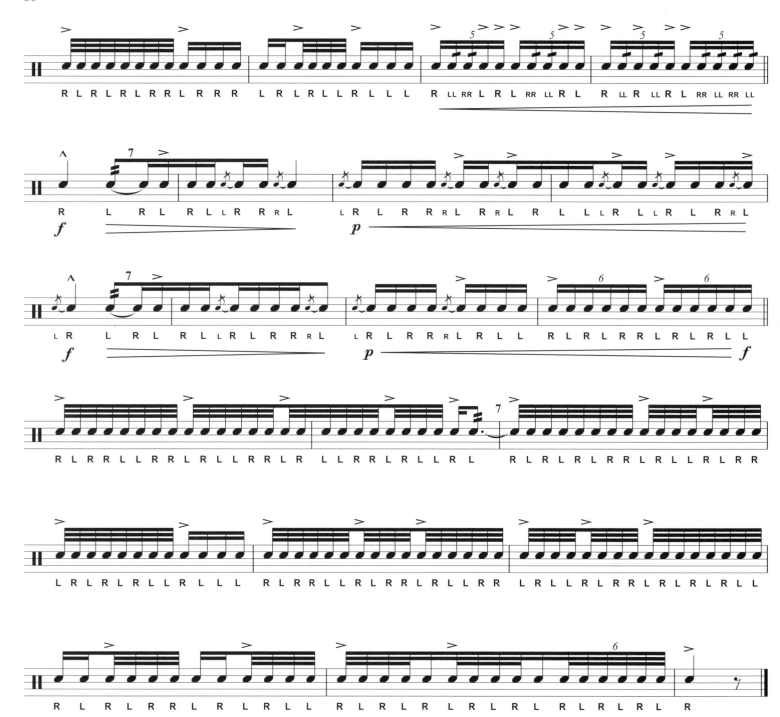

Author's Note
I believe that many drummers don't give their left hand as much credit as it deserves, so I decided to write this solo in a manner that would equally challange both hands. The source of the title may also be of interest. While visiting my friend and drum maker, Mr. Bill Reamer of East Earl, Pennsylvania, he played a video of Buddy Rich. It brought me back to my childhood when I first heard him play and I reminisced about the incredible influence he was on me, both then and now! I decided to incorporate his name into the title.